I0087126

To

From

Date

The Disruptive Power of

GRACE

BOLA CROWN

THE
CORNERSTONE
PUBLISHING

The Disruptive Power of Grace

Copyright © 2019 by **Bola Crown**

Paperback ISBN: 978-1-944652-90-6

Printed in the USA.

Author's Contact

For booking to speak at your next event or to order bulk copies of this book please sent email to bolacrownbook@gmail.com

---

Published by:
Cornerstone Publishing
A Division of Cornerstone Creativity Group LLC
Info@thecornerstonepublishers.com
www.thecornerstonepublishers.com

516.547.4999

CONTENTS

FOREWORD

———— ⚜ ————

Bola has written a narrative theology of grace. She did this without theologizing or preaching. She simply tells us a story about her life; her own self-interpretation of her journey here on earth. Her story demonstrates that there is a good God who rules the affairs of women and men in this world. Her story speaks of the power of God's favor in a Christian life. She gives us a moving story of the grace of God that abounds in her life. God is particularly kind to her. God loves her.

What is the grace of God? you may ask. We do not need to define it; we do not need to philosophize about it, and we do not need to fully grasp it to experience its work. For Bola, grace is not argued. It is not something she claims she can hold in her hands as a private-banking document; it is a lived experience of encountering the triune God at multiple levels of her existence. God meets with her at various spheres and dimensions of her life. Read her memoir and take time to meditate on the various dimensions of God's grace that her story reveals to the world.

I discerned about eight dimensions of grace. This is not because Bola likes the number 8, as she was born on August 8 and does not tire of telling me that the number 8 stands for a new beginning. Her story, as crafted in this memoir, reveals that: One, God's grace saves us as sinners and delivers us into the marvelous light of Jesus Christ, into eternal life; two, grace transforms our relationships with God, other human beings, and the world; three, grace is the divine power that makes a way for us where is no way, takes us beyond our natural abilities and learned capabilities; four, grace is the sustaining power of our spirituality, our daily walk with God; five, grace gives us a new character by renewing our minds and habits; six, the grace of God heals our physical, psychological, and spiritual wounds; seven, the grace of God gives us a second chance when we fail. God is always ready to begin with us again; and eight, grace is disruptive and irruptive. God's grace radically challenges and unsettles our human presumptions of self-sufficiency and self-complacency.

Grace is an appearance of something new into creation, human life, human condition—which breaks into the order of things. It allows freedom to appear, to flourish as such. It is a movement toward openness to futural possibilities, dislocating human lives and situations toward their future forms, nudging them toward full actualization of their potentials. Grace expresses the hidden potentials of a situation, existence or life, as well as transcends it.

Has Bola not in this narrative crafted a theology of grace? Has she not engaged in God-talk, theo-logy? Has she not described and explained God to us? Has she not given us a story of God's interaction with her? I think she has done all these—and has done them admirably well with a flowing, graceful prose.

There is something else that shines through from the midst of the eight dimensions of grace that Bola has revealed to us; something that nudges us to love, to be gracious in our dealings with other human beings. She shows us how to allow God's grace to run its full circle in our lives.

God's grace in Bola's life is not split; it forms a circle. Grace received is not estranged from grace returned, and I am naming grace returned (reciprocated) as love. Here, love is not sentimentality, but an extension of received grace from one to another. I am conceptualizing love as grace, returned grace, or the circulation of grace. Bola manifests the gratuitousness of grace in her life as the gratuitousness of love in her relationships. This is to say she manifests or returns grace as love in her relationships. Bola knows that much of what has come to her are free gifts of God and blessings from God's children who have crossed her path and she tries her best to always keep the love of God flowing in the world. For Bola, love is the disposition of persons who are grateful for having received God's grace and are thus faithful to it, engaged with it, motivated by it, and committed to extending it to others. Love is the articulation and extension of the grace one has received to others.

Let me end this foreword with a personal story, the tale of how Bola became my daughter. I first met Bola and her husband in the winter of 1998 when they came into the Pentecostal church I was pastoring. My wife and I hit off with them immediately. As I came to better know Bola, I realized that she loved her dad dearly and was concerned at the time that they were estranged. I had had a similar experience with my dad. I encouraged her to reach out to her dad and seek reconciliation. She did and became joyful that her father was once again in her life. When she was traveling to Nigeria to see him, after many years of having not set eyes on him, I gave her some gift of books to give to him.

Then this happened. I went to Nigeria in January 2006 and called Bola's mother—for Bola had given me her number and wanted me to check on her. I called and a man picked up the phone and I mentioned my name and added that: "Please, may I speak to Bola's mother?" Then the unexpected happened:

Man (with a commanding voice): "Who is this young man who wants to speak to my wife? What do you want from her?"

Me: "Bola asked me to check on her mum, Sir. I am Bola's pastor from America."

Man: "You got to speak to me first. Why do you call my wife, young man?"

Me: (Silence. I thought I had dialed the wrong number).

After this "inquisition" session, we went on to speak at length. Apparently, the man knew me, and was playing hardball with me. Bola had not told me her father had such military humor, nor had she warned me that he would be at her mother's place. He knew who I was but feigned ignorance. He knew that I was close to Bola and her husband; she had related stories about me to him, her mother, and siblings for years. It was a nice way to break the ice with the retired army colonel.

In the course of our conversation I kept referring to Bola as his daughter. Then, suddenly, in a very solemn voice, he told me: "She is now your daughter, my friend. I hand her over to you, please take good care of her for me. I am not in America, and I have handed her over to you as your daughter."

Something in that declaration and that non-repeatable kairotic moment made me realize that Bola had become my own daughter. When her own daughter arrived, I told many of my friends that my first grandchild had come. They shook their heads, knowing the tender ages of my three biological children. To relieve them of their confusion, I whispered to them that I had a grown daughter, whom they did not know, who was married to a Yoruba prince and it was all about God's grace.

Bola is not just the daughter of her biological

father; she is not just my daughter by paperless adoption - through the unquestionable fiat of an African father - she is truly God's daughter. The grace of God that has carried her this far in life will take her further and deeper into the actualization of her potentialities and to the fullest display of God's love to the whole earth.

Dr. Nimi Wariboko, MBA, PhD
Walter G. Muelder Professor of Social Ethics
Boston University, Boston, MA. USA

June 20, 2019

DEDICATION

This book is dedicated to two of the trio, my husband and my daughter. Thank you for believing in me, encouraging me, and inspiring me daily. I love you!

Also, to my wonderful siblings, this book is written in your honor. We have been through so much together! As our mother would often say, "hardship does not kill, it is comfort that that kills!"

ACKNOWLEDGMENTS

I would like to thank my husband for being my number one supporter, believing in me and never once getting in the way of my adventures. You have pushed me right from the beginning, to see the best of me come out. I know I often drive you crazy, as you do me, but know this: you were and remain the first thing on my list of getting it right!

To my "life is good" daughter, the one who put an end to mummy's tears, my answer to 15 years of prayers, you are God's gift to me. As I often say to you, if it is possible to love someone too much, then I admit that I am guilty. I love you sweetie!

To my mother, you are my inspiration in so many ways that I cannot count. Your cheerfulness, even in the face of countless hardships, is unparalleled. You are the definition of resilience and you combine it so gracefully with joy. I am proud to be your daughter!

To my dad, thank you for the gifts of oratory and poetry. I inherited your colorful ways with words and it is the reason I am able to do this.

To my wonderful siblings, we have experienced so much together and I would not trade you for any other. I love and appreciate you all!

To my wonderful second parents, my parents-in-law, thank you for making a home for me. You are amazing.

To my lovely sisters-in-law, the Opebi clan, my other sisters and brothers-in-law, nieces, nephews, and my mother's other children through paperless adoption, I love you all.

Late Colonel Lawrence Ishola Lawal, who taught Commandos integrity and class, his great legacy lives on.

Late Reverend Olapeju Oyefuga, and his wife, who proved that friendship can be as strong as blood.

Brother Ben Bere, thanks for your question; "sister Bola, where is your book?"

Sister Anne Babalola, your book inspired me!

Ayo and Dayo Arogbo, Segi and Pastor Akin Laoye, Sade Lawal Salako, Toyin Afolayan

Olaitan, Pastors Yemisi and Phillips Aladesua, the Fatungases, the Toyobos, the Arikawes, Biola and Pastor Lanre Peters, Wunmi and Pastor Laolu Akande, the Ngwabas and the Ainas, I appreciate you all.

To all my wonderful and amazing friends too numerous to mention, as I am blessed to be surrounded by so many loving friends, I appreciate you all!

Pastors Nimi and Wapaemi Wariboko, Pastors Daps and Kenny Zion, Aunty Labo Tokoya, Aunty Funmi and Uncle Sesan Ogun, Naz Vahid, Pastors Ayo and Ronke Aduroja, this book would not be complete without a special mention of you.

Pastor Paul Okolie, Pastors Kunle and Peju Omotosho, Pastor and Pastor Mrs Otokiti, Pastor Ben, thank you for your support.

Pastor Nimi, Abisola, Bimpe, Seun, Mosun and Cornerstone Publishing, thank you for the editing and production of this book. You made it possible!

CHAPTER 1

GRACE FROM THE START

I was not meant to be, but for grace! I grew up to learn of two very remarkable incidents that happened in the first few days and a few months of my life. The first incident was around the time of my birth and christening, while the second occurred when I was between six to 12 months old.

Few weeks to my birth, my father had gained admission into two universities: University of Ife, to study Law; and University of Ibadan, to study English Language. He was the first person in his family to aspire to such level of education; unfortunately, however, he did not have tuition fees for either opportunity.

As a 28-year-old man, husband, and father to a two-year-old toddler and expecting baby number two any day, it seemed as though my father's academic dream had become a mirage. Things were very dicey financially and it was a question of either taking care of his family, or going to college. But even if he were to find a way around the financial hurdle, going to college would mean leaving his young wife all by herself to care for a toddler and a newborn. How would she cope with two young kids? There was hardly enough financial support for one child, and now a second!

BEGINNING OF MIRACLES

I was born in the middle of this tension. And while there was joy at my safe arrival, there was also the obvious reality of the challenges at hand.

As is the custom in our Yoruba culture - which closely mirrors the biblical tradition, a naming ceremony was held for me on the eighth day of my birth. Also, similar to what is recorded in the Bible regarding the presentation of gifts to baby Jesus by the wise men, people who came for my christening gave my parents money and other gift items to help care for me and the family.

And so goes the story that after the ceremony was over and most of the guests had left, my mother pulled my father into the bedroom, and gave him all the money she had been given at the naming ceremony. She encouraged him to head to college that week and pay his tuition so he could begin his studies. By this time, he had settled on going to University of Ibadan, they would move from Sagamu to Ibadan, and it would be easier for him to visit home regularly. He was to study English language.

As my mother still recounts, my father was so overwhelmed by this gesture of hers that he became emotional. Tears welled up in his eyes and streamed down his face. This was raw love on display and he was blown away. She assured him that she would cope with their two daughters while he went off to school. There was some food at home, and some family members and friends would help her care for us.

When my father eventually caught his breath, all he could do was to start praying for me. He prayed that since he was using monetary gifts that were meant for my care as his school fees, God should bless me with a smart brain so that I could also go to college and be exceptional. He further wrote a poem to memorialize the events surrounding my birth and christening, including the spectacular way in which he got his first college tuition. And the romantic that he is, he could not help mentioning the great human achievement and world record of that year - 1969 - a man landing on the moon.

I believe the passionate prayer that my father offered to God was heard and answered because, many years after, in 1990, I would go on to emerge as the best graduating Law student at Ogun State University. Grace at work!

MERCY SAID NO

Still on the miracles that surrounded my birth and early life, I was told that six months after my birth, a chicken pox epidemic broke out where we lived in Elewe-Omo area of Ibadan. As a result, several children died every night in the first few months of 1970.

Somehow, I also contracted the chicken pox. And it got so bad that I was admitted into the hospital, and my parents took turns to watch over me in the ward, and some of their friends also volunteered to watch me. As I was so young, the medics had to pass food and liquid through tubes directly into my veins. Given my frailty and all the tubes, my parents were under strict instructions to hold me still. Failure to hold me still and keep all the tubes and needles in place could be deadly, they were told.

Every time I reflect on what could have been the state of medical practice in Nigeria within that period, I can only conclude that God's grace must have been at work in my life. And then I also wonder how tough it must have been for my parents, particularly my mother, who did most of it, as my father still shuttled between the hospital and the university. They had to hold me still most of the time, and sleeping would have been almost nonexistent. Such sacrifice! Such labor of love!

My mother told me that as time went on, the number of children in the hospital reduced every night. Unfortunately, it was not because the children got well and were discharged; it was because they continued to die in numbers. And then one night it happened that the doctor informed my mother, that I no longer had a pulse. The worst had finally happened – or so they thought - and I was moved out immediately.

My mother was distraught! She was inconsolable. A neighbor, who had been aware of my critical condition and had come to the hospital to assist my mother, was around when the doctor broke the sad news. She tried comforting my mother, and also sent an urgent message to my father who had been away when the news was delivered. While waiting for his arrival, the neighbor and others present with my mother, placed me in a pillow slip, tied it up and put me in the trunk of a car.

Somewhere in the middle of all this, my father arrived. My parents were encouraged to take my pulseless body to a priest for the final rites. The hospital was Catholic-owned, so they drove to the chapel and found the priest. I will never know the exact sequence of events that ensued but I was told that, at some point, the priest stopped praying and went still. He then looked down at my motionless body and said to my parents, "I think she moved!" "What?" they, blurted out in shock, their gaze fully on the priest.

And in what must have seemed like an eternity to them but which could have been just a few seconds, the priest checked my pulse. Then he said to them in disbelief, "She has a pulse!"

Immediately, my parents jumped into action and drove me back to the children's ward, looking for the doctor. This time, I was not in a pillow slip, nor in the trunk of a car; I was in the cradling arms of my loving mother who anxiously held on to me, until they were back at the children's hospital. I was under constant observation and gradually responded to treatment. I stayed for a few more months at the hospital, eventually got better and survived the chicken pox epidemic! Grace at work, yet again!

Grace disrupted the power of death and gave life, triumphing over diseases and science.

CHAPTER 2

STEPPING STONES

I am one of eight siblings. Number two, to be precise. Growing up in a middle-class Nigerian family was fun. With my father being a military officer, we had resources available to us, perhaps more than the average middle-class family. Way back when the Nigerian economy was very robust, we lived in large homes and had vehicles with drivers, in addition to other perks provided by the Nigerian Army.

However, being one of eight children meant stretching the family's resources extremely thin. Even by Nigerian standards, having eight children from one woman was on the high side. Most of my friends were from smaller families, and five kids seemed to be the average at that time.

My father's income from the Nigerian Army was the main source of sustenance for our family. My mother was a small-scale trader. She sold household items and not much came from the business. Besides, she was definitely preoccupied with raising eight children mostly by herself, as my father was often on transfer to army bases.

I recall wondering and even asking why my parents had so many children. There was no exact answer given but, anecdotally, the excuse was that my father was the only surviving child of his parents, because his father had died while he was very young. His mother, had ended up remarrying and having another son. My father thus appeared to be on a mission to ensure his father's name was never forgotten.

Another, and perhaps the more credible reason is that my mother, had given birth to just one boy out of the first five kids. In most parts of Africa, having male children has always been a big deal. So, my parents kept having more kids until they eventually had a second boy.

DIVIDED ATTENTION

In my early teenage years, our family became even larger, when my father, like many other Nigerian men in the 1980s, decided to marry another wife. This made resources very scarce as we had to share whatever was available with the extended family.

Polygamy was a phenomenon that hit many men in my father's generation. He and many other Christian men in the same age bracket took liberties and married other women without divorcing or separating from their first wives. It was a pretty common practice that had no basis in their faith or religion. Unlike their Muslim counterparts who are legally allowed to marry up to four wives, these Christian men, like my father, did it because it was culturally acceptable. Polygamy is still acceptable in Nigeria, though today's Christians are becoming less attracted to it.

In polygamous homes, the second wives are usually younger and more educated than the first. Consequently, these men focus most of their attention and devotion on the younger wives and their children. This means that there are many people my age who grew up without their fathers playing active roles in their lives. There were absentee fathers all over the place and many children grew up without their father's love. Naturally, many women had to take on the roles of both parents for their children.

THE TOUGH ONE

Growing up with such a family dynamic was rough and tough. It was toxic for the mothers who were often left to raise up the children on their own. They were neither divorced nor were they widows; so they did not even have the chance for closure. They were emotionally and physically bereft of the comfort of a marriage, yet they could not move on.

These women were saddled with the economic burdens of raising many kids mostly by themselves or with the help of family members and even strangers. Many of them had cut out of their education to raise their children; they had meager earnings from petty trading or low-level paying jobs. Many of these women were deserted after they had given their youth to raising kids and were not as attractive as they used to be. Many resorted to any means possible to cater for themselves and their children.

I recall my mother taking her most expensive clothes and jewelry and pawning them away so our school fees could be paid. Thank God for all resilient mothers like her who understood that education was the way out of poverty! The only thing that perhaps made the plight of these women somewhat bearable was the fact that they were not the only ones in the situation; cases of men abandonment were commonplace and tolerable for them.

Fortunately, as an older sibling, I had the privilege of knowing my father when he was just married to my mother. He was a devoted husband and father. Those were great times as we often had quality family time together. I recall very fondly trips to the famous Lagos Bar Beach during the holidays. But, alas, it was short-lived because my father had to share his love, time and resources with his other family.

Sometimes I feel sorry for my younger siblings as they never knew what it was to have the undivided love of a father. They always had to share him. But then I wonder if they were not better off than those of us who, because we knew what his undivided love was like, could not fully recover from the trauma of not having him around as much as we grew older – especially during the very sensitive adolescent years. And I also feel sorry for my half-siblings, because like us, they did not ask to be born into such circumstances.

It is worth noting, that we have been reconciled to our father and have a good relationship with him.

REDEEMING LOVE

With all of our childhood experiences, it became such a beautiful thing to learn about the love of God and how, as our heavenly Father, He loves us unconditionally. He is a Father that will never leave us; He will never walk out on us or desert us. It is such pure love that rather than asking for anything, He gave Himself fully to us through His Son, Jesus Christ.

Understanding the love of God helps to heal our wounds, and also empowers us to forgive. And forgiveness is a must, because forgiveness is the only path for the wounded to heal. We don't forget, and I daresay we should not forget, but we must forgive. We forgive so that we can move on and give ourselves a chance for a positive future. Otherwise, future relationships will be damaged by the wounds of yesterday.

Again, I would say to anyone who may have had a similar experience as mine, that the helplessness our mothers felt should be the reason for every woman to pursue economic independence. For some, this could mean getting further education to earn more income; for others, it could mean becoming entrepreneurs who are managing and growing their own businesses.

As mothers, we are role models for our sons and daughters on how to maintain positive relationships. We can take a cue from the woman described in Proverbs 31. That woman had economic independence, yet it did not get in the way of her family relationships. Although she had enough to buy land on her own, the Bible records that her husband and children called her blessed.

I recognize that women may not be able to accomplish it all at the same time, but I also believe it does not have to be one or the other. You do not have to choose being a wife or mother over economic independence. I believe you can do both, and one just has to have the wisdom and grace to balance things out. This is where the grace of God comes in - to know when and how to pay attention to different areas of our lives.

CHAPTER 3
GRACE OVERFLOW

For as long as I can remember, I was a procrastinator, and someone who almost always took things for granted. I never really pushed myself and I definitely stretched the hand of grace.

I recall once coming first in my class while in primary (elementary) school without an ounce of effort. Like my mother, I am blessed with a powerful memory that captures, stores and retains information very well; hence I was often able to recall things I was taught in class without much studying. So when I took the first position in my fourth grade, my father was quite happy, but his dear friend of blessed memory, Mr. Adeyemi who was a teacher and was often in our house, pulled him aside and gave him this candid advice: "For this girl to come first without studying, it means the school is not good enough. Take her to a school that will challenge her." And that was how I was transferred from

Army Children School to Command Children School.

Mr. Adeyemi was right - I was definitely challenged in my new school, and my next grade rating was in double digits. That should have been a wakeup call for me to put in more effort in my studies but I guess I was too young to figure it all out at that time.

I must confess that this casual attitude trailed me throughout my education, including my time at the law school. To be fair, though, I had some experiences that can be said to have contributed to or, at least, reinforced this attitude of mine. A particular experience in my first year of high school readily comes to mind. I went to a boarding school called Command Secondary School, located in Ipaja, a suburb of Lagos. Incidentally, boarding school has always been a popular choice in Nigeria. It was particularly common in the 80s and 90s for wealthy and middle-class families to have their children between the ages of 11 and 17 go to boarding schools. We were meant to learn independence from our parents and families, as well as the ability to survive outside the comforts of our homes. I believe going to a boarding school was a good foundation which definitely helped when I migrated to the United States.

The experience I mentioned earlier while I was in my first year had to do with studying. I often saw many of my classmates and roommate studying late at night. This was new to me; and I also saw how the senior girls in our dorm room praised these girls. I liked the idea of being praised, so I decided to join some of my classmates to study at night. Well, it turned out that I got the worst grades of my life that year. My grades were so poor that even I was disappointed in myself. I might never have really cared about grades, but I at least had some subconscious expectations for my school performance. I never thought I could perform as poorly as my results showed in that first year.

Looking back now, I can rightly pinpoint a number of factors that could have led to the poor results, including being away from home and in a school far away from my loved ones. But I simply blamed it all on the fact that I studied at night, trying to be like other students. As an 11-year-old, my logic was that my school performance was much better when I did not study. So why study?

WONDERS OF SELF-AWARENESS

It is interesting that my grades did improve after that first year and got better over the years in high school. I studied more as I got older but mostly during the day, almost never at night. I have since come to realize that the reason I did poorly in my first year was because I really did not learn anything, even though I stayed up like some of my classmates.

As I grew older and got to understand more about myself, I realized that I learn more during the day. I am a morning person and my most productive time is in the morning. Although I did the motions of staying up and studying at night, I did not really learn anything but rather punished myself with sleep deprivation, which eventually impaired my attention level in class the next day. My listening abilities were negatively impacted by lack of good sleep and I ended up with overall poor performance.

Over the years, however, I came to realize that what would take me fifteen minutes to read and understand in the day time, would take me at least thirty minutes at night. I am generally slower as the day wears on.

It is very important that we know enough about ourselves so we can optimize and maximize our abilities and potentials. This frees us from the desperation to bow to peer pressure or try to please others to our own detriment.

Much later, in my thirties, I realized that I am also more productive in the morning at everything else, and not just studying. So now I try to do my most important work in the morning, make important decisions in the morning and on and on it goes. I also try to avoid idle chats in the morning with people who like to chat in the morning - night people.

I learned this the hard way through a colleague at work who has now become a personal friend. Whenever she arrived at work, her natural propensity was to chat everybody up, telling them what happened in her household the night before. She did this every morning and I would gladly oblige her by listening to her chatter. It took me a while to realize that my friend was built differently from me. On the few occasions that I tried to chat her up in the evening, when I felt the day was wrapping up, and it was okay to chat, she was usually non-communicative. She would respond in mono syllables at most. Gradually, I realized that her productive time was at night - and she had little or no time for small chats at that time.

What a revelation that was! Once I understood what was going on, I brought it up to my friend's attention and we agreed that we would both respect each other's zone. We agreed to a time midday when we could both chat. She would respect my morning time and I would respect her evening time. That certainly saved the friendship!

TIMELY INTERVENTION

When I gained admission into Ogun State University (now Olabisi Onabanjo University), I was offered English Language, but my father wanted me to study Law; so, there were expectations that I could switch to Law in my second year. I did nothing special on my end to make this happen as I partied away in my first year. Fortunately, my grades were good enough that I was able to cross over to Law.

I think my father wanted me to study Law so he could vicariously accomplish what he could not do himself. I mentioned earlier that he had been admitted to study Law at the University of Ife, but had been unable to do so due to lack of funds. Today, he is the proud father of four lawyers!

I will always be thankful that my father pushed me to become a lawyer. Growing up, I certainly was a precocious child, always questioning everything and not afraid to challenge supposed norms. I recall that, at home, my father would always have special meals made for him, and he had a special seat at the dining table. Once I said to my mother, "Why do you cook special meals for Daddy? Aren't we his kids and shouldn't we also get the same perks? We should all eat the same thing."

I don't think my mother responded, as she had been too shocked by the sheer guts I had to even dare to ask. Of course, my father heard and his reaction was to say, "This girl will become a lawyer, so she can go to court and question people." He was apparently referring to TV programs that would show a lawyer examining or cross-examining a witness. For him that would be the best use of my talent.

So, I did become a lawyer but never practiced Law. Instead, I found myself in banking and it has been a fun ride ever since.

GRACE TO THE RESCUE

Out of ignorance, I most certainly pushed the concept of "just enough" to its limits. For instance, in my first-year finals, there was an exam that I took in which I concluded, without bothering to answer all the necessary questions, that I had done enough to pass. I left the last few questions unanswered because I stupidly believed it was not cool to ace a test. I wanted the bragging rights to say, "I did enough to pass but who needs to get 100?!"

Such was the depth of my ignorance! Such a shame! As I will be revealing shortly, this bad attitude almost caught up with me later. So glad that grace saved me!

Again, while in my third year studying Law, one of the other students staying in the same private home we rented told me he believed I could make a first-class degree if I spent more time on my studies and less on arguing and clowning around. I proudly replied him that I had no ambition of making a first class, which, in my opinion, was for nerds and boring people. I now know better. It is not really about getting the highest grade possible but more about not living below one's potential.

Jesus shared about talents in the Bible. He used a parable to explain that God does not demand the same level of performance from each of us. Instead, it is about what we do with what He has given us. He was equally pleased with the person who turned two talents into four, and the person who turned five talents into ten. God's reaction to both of them was the same because they both doubled what they had been given. It is not about how much you do (quantity), but what you do with how much you are given (quality). To the person who was given one and did nothing with it, God took the one from him and gave it to the person who had ten. This is why it is unwise to compare ourselves with other people. We have different destinies, and God's expectations of each of us are not necessarily the same.

As I mentioned earlier, I was always a last-minute person when it came to studies, so I am thankful that I was able to pull things off. In my final year, I had a clash with one of my friends who walked me out of her room while a few of us were studying. Her grouse with me was that I always seemed to have better grades than her, although I did not study as much, or did a crash study or manic last-minute studying.

While I was not sure how to remedy that, it just seemed like she had tired of me. I think that incident propelled me to study harder than I usually would have done. This significantly helped to boost my grades and eventually led me into graduating as the best graduating Law student of Ogun State University in 1990. I cannot take much personal credit for that feat but to acknowledge that it was grace at work.

NARROW ESCAPE

After graduating from college, I went on to the Nigerian Law School, Lagos, for professional law studies. I was fortunate to have private accommodation with an uncle who lived close to the school. I shared a room with another relative of his, called Bunmi.. While in the school, I took a lot for granted and carried on with my usual casual attitude and left studying to the last minute. This time, however, it seemed the chickens had finally come home to roost. My lack of discipline had finally reached its limits!

It was very late in the game that it dawned on me that, as the best graduating Law student from my college, it was imperative that I did well in law school, not just for myself but also to represent my college. This was the first time I had to take other people's interests into consideration. I can't actually recall how I came to this realization; but it's most likely that one of my classmates had thrown subtle jabs at me.

With law school examinations a number of weeks away, I realized I was in trouble and started to panic. It crossed my mind that I had left things too late and I became really desperate. One evening, as I started to cry and lament my fate, my roommate, Bunmi, heard me and decided to cheer me up. You see, Bunmi happened to be a born-again Christian, and when she saw how panicky I was as the final examinations drew closer, she became a source of encouragement. By this time, two of my friends had joined me in my uncle's apartment. This way, we could all study together, as I was the one living closest to law school.

One day, Bunmi mentioned to my friends and me the concept of "prayer of agreement". This was foreign to me. I had never heard of it as I was just a nominal Christian who hardly went to church. Bunmi explained that a prayer of agreement is based on the biblical principle that if two or more people agree on a matter and pray about it, God would answer. This stems from Jesus' assurance that wherever two or more people come together in His name, He would be there in their midst.

Desperate as I was, I was willing to try this concept. So, Bunmi, Lara, Funmi and I prayed together. And then I began to study in earnest. Thankfully, God answered and honored that prayer. We all made 2:2. While it was a drop from my 2:1 grade in college, it still felt good that I did not disgrace myself, my family or my college. Phew!

Looking back, I know I could have done much better. And I hope sharing this encourages someone out there to push themselves a little more. You are the ultimate beneficiary of your hard work!

CHAPTER 4
SAVING GRACE

My first job was in a bank, and it was going on fine; I was learning new things every day. I had recently broken up with my boyfriend and was in a phase of questioning things. I was happy but felt there had to be more.

In my usual way of expressing and unburdening myself, I got my pen and wrote what I titled "My Many Lives". In that write-up, I broke my life into sections and summed up my life in each. The sections were: My family life, my work life, my love life and my faith life. The first two were known and defined. My love life was in flux. My faith life was nonexistent.

I considered it necessary to reflect, appreciate and recognize that so much had been going well for me, not because I deserved or earned it but because of divine providence. At this point in my life, it was obvious that these were not mere coincidences. My life had been threatened, yet I survived. I had been carefree about education, yet I had done excellently well.

Even my job at the time was nothing short of a miracle. In Nigeria, to get a banking job, you either had to have come from a well-known family or had a known godfather or uncle. Regardless of your qualifications, you would still need to know the right people to get such a plum job. It did not just happen. In my case, my father was retired from the army at this time, and he did not know many people in the banking industry.

Fortunately, I had been in touch with a few friends from high school. One of them was dating the daughter of an influential man. Somehow, this guy got to know that I was in need of a job and the information got to his girlfriend, and she then told her father. Next thing you know, I received a letter which I presented to the CEO of the bank. I will never forget his remarks after he read the letter, "You are from Uncle?" The only thing I could do was nod, because I had never met this "uncle" and I prayed silently that the CEO would not ask me any other questions. Thankfully, he didn't. And that was how I landed my first job!

So, reflecting on my faith life, I felt it was time to give God His rightful place in my life. If God had been so gracious to me, the least I could do was show gratitude by becoming dedicated to Him. I had asked Jesus to be my Lord and Savior in the past but had not really meant it. This time was different, though. I had come to realize that I could not take the grace of God for granted. Thankful for what Jesus had done for me, I asked Him to forgive my sins and become my Lord. I was changed.

It is not that I immediately stopped sinning or became perfect but I had Jesus as my Lord to forgive and clean me up; to lead and direct me. I no longer needed to be desperate for the affirmation of men. That desperation had led me into making some mistakes in the past, seeking for love in the wrong places and from the wrong people. In Jesus I found true love and peace. I knew I had a God who cared about everything concerning me and would also take care of my tomorrow. I was thankful and I remain thankful for His love.

LIBERATING JOURNEY

And so, I began my faith walk with baby steps. Learning, making mistakes and learning again. It has been a great ride knowing Jesus and loving Him through His words in the Bible, praying to Him, seeking His guidance. I once read somewhere that Christians are not perfect, but are rather fully aware of their imperfections, which makes them turn to Jesus for help.

My first boss, Mr Olusola Arogbo of blessed memory, was an early example of what I call attractive Christianity. A Christianity that made others to say, "I want what he has!" He radiated joy and confidence through his faith in God. He took his work seriously and was conscious that he had a destiny to reflect the love of God.

In my new relationship with God, I started to gain more confidence in myself because I started to see myself as God saw me. In the Bible, He calls us the apple of His eyes. He loves us so much that He chose to die for us. He also chose to love us; we did not and could not earn His love. So, we can rest assured that His love for us is not based on our performance; it is based on His choice to love us.

How liberating it is to know that I could never do anything to qualify or disqualify myself from God's love! As long as I continue to seek to do His will, He will always love me! It is the deep understanding of His love that gives me joy that I would never be able to fully put in words.

THE GODSEND

Woven into this love story is someone God used among many others in my faith walk. Around the time I wrote about my many lives, I started getting close to a young man who was also in my office and we soon became close friends. Incidentally, we had attended the same college but were not on the same campus. We had started at the bank on the same day and I recall several people asking if I knew him, to which I replied in the negative.

It turns out, as I would later learn from him, that our paths had crossed once or twice while in college. He told me of the first time as he could recall it quite vividly. Interestingly, I could also recall the incident but, until then, I had not been able to remember any of the faces.

It had been our matriculation day and my parents had to leave early to go home. They would have dropped me at my off campus apartment, but I told them I would wait for my friends who were still on campus. So, off they went while I hung around with my friends. A while later, I realized that my friends were not ready to head back to our apartment, so I decided to head home alone.

While waiting to catch a taxi, a car stopped by and the glass rolled down. Instinctively, I stepped back and waved off to the driver to indicate that I was not getting in. Still, he asked, "Where are you going?" No response. Then I saw the back window begin to roll down and at the same time heard the man behind the steering asking me to look into the car as there were two other people like me in it. He said he only stopped because I was holding a matriculation gown. He said it looked like I was heading in the direction of his sister and nephew, and would be happy to drop me off.

Seeing that the two people in the back were young like me and that they also had matriculation gowns, I got into the car. The young man whom my benefactor referred to as his nephew is the same person I described as my friend earlier. He was first a friend, who soon became my Bible teacher. Much later, he became my fiancé and eventually my husband.

With hindsight, I now know that our seemingly coincidental first meeting then had been divinely arranged. But then, it was not until five years later that our paths crossed again at the bank. And although I could remember the car incident, I could not remember his face or that of his uncle who had driven the car. He, on the other hand, surely remembered both the incident and my face. To this day, I kid him that I must have left quite an impression for him to remember that vividly.

While in school, though, we were both in different social circles. That significantly affected the possibility of our running into each other. Moreover, seeing as we were both in our teenage years - very young and yet to figure things out - I believe God did not let our paths cross more often because our friendship had been designed for a future time when we would have become more mature.

In any case, since I was not a Christian at that time, there could have been nothing more to spark the flames of friendship between us. He had become a born-again Christian while in college, while I did not even go to church.

Thankfully, God brought us together at the right season in my life when I was seeking Him. So, he was a friend who helped guide me along as I tried to understand the Bible and what it meant to be a Christian. Oh, the joy of knowing and learning something bigger than you!

Within the period that our relationship started,

I observed that it was not like any I had known in the past. This was not a physical, sexual relationship. It was different, and I had to learn building a relationship that was deeper in nature because we could not use sex as a cover up. All of our humanity was on display and we had to learn to understand each other under God's guidance, and trust that He was leading us in the relationship. Several times, there were clashes of wills. I had to learn a new way of love. It had its own challenges but I never had to question if it was sex that kept the relationship going. We both had to learn to trust God to guide us.

TAKING THE BIG LEAP

I was very new to this born-again thing and learning to trust God to choose what is best for you, rather than making your own choices. So, when it came to the issue of marriage, I understood that I could not just choose who I wanted but had to pray and ask God to choose for me.

On my part, I asked God for two things in the man he would choose for me. First, he had to love God; second, he had to be intelligent. While I had other Christian brothers showing interest in me, I think what attracted me to my husband in particular was and remains his love for God. He was uncompromising in his faith. It was either the God way or no way at all.

Embedded in that disposition is a strong character and great integrity. That was quite refreshing for me as I had met many men who were so flippant in declaring affection and never meaning it. All they were after was getting into bed with you and once that was done, you became one of their many conquests.

Surprisingly at the start of our relationship, I found myself being the person that was put on notice. He told me flat out that there would be no sex before marriage. This put me on the defensive and got me frankly offended. Yes, I might be new in the things of God, but I was also serious about my newfound faith. And, no, I was not looking to pull anyone into sin.

Notwithstanding, this marked the beginning of boundaries in our relationship and we were both clear about what was acceptable and what was not. We were in courtship for three years and then got married. It has been God and will remain God for us. Indeed, getting married to my husband made me to see his love for God in a deeper dimension. And that has helped me to love and respect him even more.

CHAPTER 5
NEW HORIZONS

After a few years of marriage and working, we got an opportunity to migrate to the United States. My husband was initially reluctant as we were both doing well in our banking careers, and there was the concern about starting all over again in another country. Interestingly, he had previously lived in the U.S. with his parents and had briefly attended Santa Monica College, in California.

We eventually decided to take the opportunity and the major reason was the prospect of accessing better medical care to assist us with fertility treatments. So, in a way, our desire to become parents brought us to the United States. Besides, we considered that it would be good for our careers to have international experiences.

And just like that, grace made it possible for a girl who had never entered an airplane before to obtain a green card while in Nigeria (note, not a visiting visa or visa lottery, but the famous

American green card) for her first trip outside of Nigeria!

I know you are wondering how that is possible. Well, as I already said, grace made it so! You see, my husband's parents, being American citizens, had filed immigration forms for their children to join them in the U.S. This was long before I met my husband and I cannot really recall when I found out about the filing. He was eventually invited for the immigration interview after we got married, and I was automatically eligible to apply as his wife. So, grace had been working things out long, long before I showed up on the scene. What I could never have considered possible, God made possible.

Permit me to say it again. The very first time I saw the inside of a plane was for a flight to the United States of America, as a green card holding legal resident! Boy, am I thankful for my parents-in-law or what?!

AGONY OF WAITING

15 years! Yes, that was how long it took us to become parents.

Words cannot describe the pain of wanting something so desperately and knowing it is ultimately not within your control. As the years rolled by, we went from anxiety to fear, to anger, to despair, to hopelessness. Then we rolled back and forth from hope to hopelessness and the cycle continued for years.

Monthly, the anguish returned. Some months were worse than others. Mother's Day became the worst day for me every year. I learned to hide my tears and master fake smiles.

I must say, though, that through it all, my husband remained my rock. While he was sad, he never questioned God. I saw his faith in action. I am thankful that I did not have to face the additional despair of him leaving for another woman. This is very common in African communities. In fact, even if a man never had such intention, family members and close friends would suggest it and continue to pressure him to take the step. So, the woman is not just dealing with infertility, but also societal pressures that she has no control over. Worse still is that it really does not matter what the root cause of infertility is, the woman gets blamed for it.

My heart goes out to women who are having to endure such pain. It is bad enough that they have to endure the horror of childlessness; but it is far unthinkable that their husbands would desert them in such agonizing circumstances. May God comfort all who are going through such predicament!

The coping mechanism for me was to rest in God's love. Although there were many times I was down and sad, I was always reminded of God's love. I knew God loved me, so although I could not fully understand the reason for infertility, I found comfort in knowing that God loved me. It was the only way to bear the pain.

My family, in-laws, friends and pastors were great sources of support and strength throughout this period. A particular friend stood out for her undying concern for me. Yemisi Aladesua (sister Yemisi as I often call her) was tireless in her love. She never stopped calling to check on me every so often. It did not matter that I hardly called her, she stayed in touch. A lesson for all of us who wonder how to nurture friendships that may appear one sided. When a friend is going through difficult times, the best gift we can give is to show that we care. We should not expect that they will reciprocate our actions, and we should not take offense if they seem to rebuff us. Without walking in their shoes, we cannot fully understand their pain. However, we can be there for them by never giving up.

Lastly, it is worth noting that throughout the ups and downs of trying to become a mother, I refused to suspend my joy. For me, it was important to remain my positive, cheerful self. I refused to allow the desire for a child to define my state of mind. So, no one could me see me and say I was not living my life. My philosophy was and remains that God is a good God, and He would do what He wants to do, when He wants to do it. So, I was not going to "pend" my life. I chose to live my life in fullness.

MAXIMIZING MY POTENTIAL

One of the ways that I decided to make the most of my life within the waiting period was to throw myself into my work. I decided to discard self-limiting habits and assumptions that had been a part of me for so long. I grew up in an environment where procrastination was the norm, and in a culture where disregard for time is common. This problem is pervasive in Africa, so much that there is a concept called "African time". This basically means "no time at all", as people can show up hours after a designated time and it is culturally acceptable, especially at social events. This was what I grew up with and what I knew.

I would say the only exception is when it comes to work. Most of us would try not to be late for work because that is our source of livelihood. But, for almost everything else, the majority of people would show up late.

You can then imagine my surprise when I realized that my friend, who would later become my husband, had a unique approach and attitude towards managing time. An approach that went beyond work. He actually expected me to be punctual when I visited or when we went out. It was quite a culture shock and a source of many misunderstandings between us when we first met. And it was clear that he was not going to succumb to the lower standard.

As I soon discovered, rooted in that quality of keeping to time are a lot of other virtues like ambition, drive, integrity and character. With time, my husband started to positively influence me in these areas.

And then I met Pastor Nimi Wariboko! Pastor Nimi was our pastor for over nine years. In him I found another Nigerian who values time. Another man of character and integrity. I thus became sandwiched between my husband and my pastor. And, naturally, my value system started to change. It was no longer good just to do enough. Mediocrity was not acceptable. Average was not good enough. I was made to know that, as a Christian, my work is a reflection of my faith. So, it had to be excellent for God to get the glory.

You will recall how I left an examination uncompleted because I felt I had done enough to pass. For these two men, however, that was unheard of. Totally unacceptable. Again, the parable of the talents is an important reference point here because it is all about maximizing one's potential. Not comparing oneself with another person but making the most of what one has been given. I started to change, respecting time and understanding that my word is my bond.

PARADIGM SHIFT

I recall that within just a few years of working with Pastor Nimi as a minister in church, he pulled me aside one day and said he was concerned about me. "Sister Bola, I'm concerned about you," he said. "I'm concerned that you want to live below your potential."

Deja vu! Recall that I mentioned earlier about the college friend who told me that if I had spent the same amount of time I spent arguing on studying, I could make a first class. And my reaction then was not one of appreciation as I thought, "Who wants to graduate summa cum laude? That is for losers!" Obviously, I did not appreciate his unsolicited advice

So, back to Pastor Nimi, his concern was certainly familiar and it rang true. He then proceeded to ask me to write an essay for and against why I would not live below my potential. Seriously? "This is laughable," I thought. "Me, a grown woman, married and doing well by many standards, to write an essay about living up to my potential?"

But then, I remembered that my husband had made the same observations to me at other times. So, I decided to take Pastor Nimi's assignment seriously. I wrote "for" and "against" why I would not live below my potential. That exercise was life-transforming for me. I encountered a paradigm shift. And I am so thankful for it. I am thankful to God, thankful to Pastor Nimi, thankful to my husband and thankful to all others God used to open my eyes to strive to attain excellence.

Our God is an excellent God. We should all aspire to be excellent. We should all maximize our God-given potential. Indeed, since I came to this realization and imbibed the philosophy, I have seen remarkable advancements in my career. I can confidently say that taking myself more seriously, honoring time, becoming disciplined and procrastinating much less have all paid off. God has taken me to heights in my career well beyond my imagination. And I remain grateful.

This is what grace has done. This is what grace can do. This is what grace continues to do!

CHAPTER 6

SURVIVING CANCER

A fter having struggled with infertility, two miscarriages, fibroids, surgeries, and other medical procedures, it came as a shock to me when I got that phone call in March 2008.

That day had been like any normal work day. I had been working late, which was not unusual. And then my husband had called, asking when I would be coming home. I replied that I did not know, to which he responded, "Come home".

There was something in his voice that I had never heard before that made me drop everything and head home immediately. We share the same family doctor, and for some reason, I had recently missed one or two annual physical checkups. Well, let's just say it was because I had been too busy and quite frankly, I had also become tired of seeing doctors because of the many hassles of the fertility treatments.

I had finally gone for the checkup in 2008, after

maybe a two-year hiatus. It was the result of my tests that our doctor had called my husband about. He could not tell me directly as I had not been at home. Besides, he needed someone to help break the news.

I had noticed a small growth around my throat but had not gone to the doctor until I had my physical that year. They had done a biopsy and, apparently, the result had not been good.

When I got home and my husband shared the news with me, I was stupefied. What? Cancer? From where and why? Was infertility not bad enough? Why cancer? The questions kept rattling me. I was numb. Almost emotionless. And then they said I had to go and see an oncologist right away for more tests.

FAITH REAWAKENED

As can be easily guessed, the next few days were surreal for me. But, then, right in the depths of my dismay and despair, I recalled an incident in January 2008 when a pastor friend had asked to pray with us for conception. Incidentally, Pastor Joseph Onigbinde also happens to be a medical doctor, and we addressed him as Dr. Onigbinde. We gladly accepted his offer to pray and he had come over to our house. While praying, Dr. Onigbinde had suddenly said, "I come against every evil in the month of March". I had considered it a bit strange that he had mentioned a particular month but I had said amen all the same. After that, I had noted it in my journal but had thought nothing more of it until that night in March.

I reminded my husband about the incident but he did not seem to recollect. So, I asked him to call Dr. Onigbinde. Dr. Onigbinde kindly accepted to accompany us to the oncologist the next day. While waiting, I reminded him about what he had said in January. He could not recollect, either. And with that came a major reassurance for me - that it had not been the pastor making things up. The fact that he could not remember was a confirmation that God had spoken through him then. In fact, I had to go back to my journal to confirm, since neither the pastor nor my husband could recall the prayer. Thankfully, I had it written in black and white, clearly dated. It had not been my imagination.

I drew a lot of confidence in the fact that God had sent His word in advance, and since this did not catch God by surprise, I held on tight believing that God would heal me. By the way, it is worth noting that Dr. Onigbinde himself had miraculously survived a rare and dangerous form of brain cancer over a decade prior. He is one of the few survivors of the particular type. Looking back, the divine order of God was apparently at work. I had only met him a few months before his visit to our place. And God used a cancer survivor to pray and send a word of healing into the future!

FORETASTE OF VICTORY

I went to work two days after the shocking news and moved around like a zombie. I had just been promoted to the role of private banker the month before and now this. My team had an offsite that week, and it was my first banker offsite, so I wanted to attend, mostly to serve as a distraction. There was nothing I could do except to pray and arrange for the surgery to be scheduled. I did not want to mope around the house, imagining crazy scenarios. So, work was a helpful distraction for me.

After a whole day of conferences and presentations, the team went off to a bowling place as a team-building, networking event. I had never bowled before, so I just sat there moping around, watching my colleagues bowl. Then I had an out-of-body experience, with me telling myself, "What am I doing here? This is the last place I should be!"

My colleagues were laughing, giggling and joking around. Most did not know what was going on with me. Only two or three of my colleagues knew. I was confused. How does one act or react at a time like this? No answer, just silence. Silence, which was often broken by the cheers from the winning side.

Incidentally, while the oncologist was conducting the tests on me the day before and talking about next steps, I had muttered to her that I did not understand why this should happen to me. Her response was swift, and it quickly brought me to life. She said, "Why not?" And then she added that most people who came to her ask, the same question and that those who focused on that, rather than focus on getting healed, didn't often do well.

That comment snapped me out of my numbness. It was as if someone had poured cold water on me. Immediately, I decided I was going to focus on getting healed. No self-pity. No pity-party. Just pray and focus on healing.

So here I was the next day at a work bowling event. Just sitting down, thinking, watching.

All of a sudden, two colleagues came to me and asked why I was not participating. I said I didn't know how to bowl. They replied, "It's easy. Come join us." Instinctively, I declined but after some persuasion, I reluctantly got up. And as I did, I heard a voice ask in my head, "What are you doing?" Too late, I was already on the floor and I was being taught how to hold the ball. Really?!

The good thing was that those two colleagues that came to me, did not know what was going on, so they treated me normally. And it felt good to ignore the fear and terrible thoughts. I swung. The ball rolled by and nothing fell. My colleagues cheered me and asked me to try again. I did. Maybe two pins fell. I gave up and started to head back to my seat. My colleagues refused, they insisted that I played another round.

So, I stayed on the floor playing. Just then, the gravity of things hit me again - a surreal moment, with a voice in my head saying I should be sitting down, I should be crying, I should be home, I should be sad. Yet there I was doing the complete opposite. It did not make sense. I guess that is faith. The Bible says faith is the substance of what you are still hoping for, the evidence of what you don't yet see.

Really, faith does not make sense. I am an attorney. The law of evidence is all about proofs and tangibles. Yet the Bible talks about evidence that is not seen. That is faith. I am thankful for the special supply of faith God gave me at that time. It was supernatural faith. A strong will that I know I do not possess normally, but God gave me such huge faith for what I was going through. And he also sent people like Pastor Onigbinde and Sister Maureen Omoaghe to pray ahead. I am grateful.

Back to bowling, it was my turn again, and I found myself silently praying to God to give me a sign. I wanted a strike. I who had never bowled before, I wanted to knock it all out. I wanted a sign that all would be okay, that I would be fine. And if it took a bowling strike, I would take it. Lord, please give me a sign.

First throw, only two pins down. And then it was time to do it again, so I threw the ball. And it rolled down unevenly. I prayed, "Lord, please help me to strike." And boom! They all went down! What?! I started jumping up and down. I leaped as high as my body could go. I was elated. At the same time, I heard that voice again in my head asking if I was okay. "How could you be jumping and smiling when just two days ago you heard the worst news of your life? How could you act as though everything was normal?"

Yes, what I was doing was not normal but I loved doing it. I silently thanked God! And hope and faith collided in that moment; I chose to believe that all would be well. I am grateful for life!

HUMAN PILLARS

Soon after, the process began. Stage two thyroid cancer. Surgery right as soon as possible. Prayers, prayers and prayers. We did not tell many people. Somehow, when people heard, most of them reacted with fear which then made me fearful. So, we decided not to tell many people, going by Pastor Nimi's advice. I also decided not tell my parents, siblings or in-laws. My parents and siblings were all in Nigeria and I did not see how telling them would help but it would certainly get them very worried.

Thank God for a community of friends, coworkers and family members, who stood by me throughout this period: Pastor Onigbinde, Pastor Nimi, Pastor Wapaemi, Naz Vahid, Geeta Madan, Einat Sadka, Sophia Bultitude, Pastors Ayo and Ronke Aduroja, Tope Atumoyongo,

Pastor and Pastor Mrs. Oyesile, Pastors Lanre and Abiola Peters, Bisola Rotimi Omodehin, Lynda Valenzuela and Debbie Marquez, doctors and nurses. And above all, my dear husband, who stood like a rock. If he had been fearful, he certainly must have hidden it from me. He was there physically, emotionally, and mentally. Hospital runs back and forth. So, so thankful to everyone.

One very interesting fact in all this is the timing of my mother,'s visit to the U.S. It was to be her first visit and we had purchased her ticket months before we found out about the diagnosis. Surprisingly, the surgery was scheduled for a day before she arrived. God, in His infinite mercies, made it possible for her visit to coincide with the time I would need her help and support. By the time I arrived from the hospital days later, she was home and waiting for me. We kept the cause of the surgery from her but she could see enough to know that it was a major procedure.

Subsequently, I had a barrage of radiation, scans and many, many hospital visits. And to God alone be the glory, He healed me, cleaned me up and made me cancer-free. I am forever grateful.

CHAPTER 7

THEN SHE CAME!

A fter overcoming such a life-challenging situation, I knew things would never be the same again. I could never see things the same way again. Everything has changed. I remain ever so thankful for life. I try to see the good in everyone and every situation, I force myself to forgive offences, and I've learned not to make big deals out of things. Life, after all, is the ultimate gift. Without life we have nothing, and with life, we have everything.

After my healing, in looking back, I was shocked that throughout the treatment, I did not pray to have children. Before that time, I had always thought that my life's biggest challenge was childlessness. I had always thought that once I had children my life would be perfect. So, I was taken aback when the desire to be a mother suddenly became a minor thought.

Indeed, everything in life is about context. What looked so big and important could suddenly become minor in a different context. My whole approach to having children changed. Although I still wanted to be a mother, I realized I could live a fulfilled life without children.

This was a paradigm shift for me. And given all the medical treatment I had recently undergone, I decided to give up on fertility treatments. No more injections, no more medications, no more mood swings, no more sudden weight gains, and no more miscarriages.

UNCOMMON INSPIRATION

With that decision came an amazing amount of freedom. Freedom to be myself. This was my decision and it felt really good. So, if I still wanted to be a mother, there was only one other option for me - adoption.

An encounter with a young adult actually helped me arrive at this decision. My boss's daughter, Leila, a young teenager, was visiting her mother, at work, and she had stopped by to say hello. I don't remember how the conversation got there, but I recall her being surprised that I was not a mother. When I told her we had been trying, she responded with such beautiful innocence that only the young and carefree could muster, "Bola, I think you should adopt, you would be a great mother."

Those words were spoken with such pureness that the message sank deep into my soul. It resonated so deeply as if I had never heard of adoption before. Of course, I had, but I had dismissed the idea every time, until now. It was probably a combination of the conviction in her words, the place I was in my life at that time, and most importantly, because she herself had been adopted. It just felt right. And I will forever be grateful to Leila for being the voice that liberated my mind to pursue adoption.

MORE LESSONS IN WAITING

When I got home that day, I shared the experience with my husband. He had no reaction. Naively, I had assumed he would have the same Eureka moment I had but it did not happen that way. It took two years of talking, waiting and convincing. Then one morning, during our morning prayers, he said, "Lord, there's something we are thinking about adopting a child. We really don't know much about it, please help us."

That was the turning point for us. And the beginning of a process that would take years, lots of money on getting vetted, and the most ridiculous amount of paperwork anyone could think of. On and on it went. There were many times we were tempted to give up on the process but we pulled through. In fact, we took a vacation to complete one set of documents.

Documents completed and turned in; home study approved trainings completed. And then the wait began. Yes, we had to wait again. In fact, this time, the wait was probably worse. Unlike fertility treatment in which we, at least, were doing some things, once you complete the adoption documentation, the rest was completely out of your hands. Did anyone check our profile, are people even making inquiries about us? It was radio silence from the agency.

ANSWERED PRAYER

Coincidentally, one of my colleagues at work, Alice, mentioned to me that she knew someone who was on the board of a Catholic adoption agency. She introduced me to him, and after lunch with Joe, he felt comfortable enough to introduce me to the agency.

Alice and Joe were angels in human form that God used as links to connect us to our angel, our princess, the one God used to bring an end to my midnight tears. The one who is the answer to our prayers. The journey of fifteen years was suddenly over. And she was young enough that we witnessed her take her first steps. And many other firsts.

May God bless Leila Ahdieh, Alice Ogrady, and the late Joe McGlaughlin's family. May God bless us and our princess. May God bless every family still waiting to experience the joy of parenthood. May your prayers be answered!

I must admit that adoption may have been easier for me because I saw people like my mother and Reverend and Mrs Olapeju Oyefuga model selfless love. They adopted (paperless adoption) non-biological children, and treated them like their own children. I saw my mother love other children unreservedly, so I knew it was possible. Also, there are several examples in the Bible like that of Moses, Esther and most definitely, Jesus Christ, who had been adopted by his stepfather, Joseph.

CHAPTER 8

FAITH AT WORK

O ne area where I have seen grace in raw display is my work. When we arrived in the U.S., my husband and I got our first jobs working in a bank as temporary staff. It was a great transition for me because I had worked with financial institutions as a customer service representative, and was fortunate enough to work with my former employer in Nigeria, Diamond Bank. I recall being able to talk to many of my former colleagues who were calling us for correspondent banking services.

I really cannot talk about my work experience in the U.S. without singling out two women. Ellen Hope was a woman I met while being interviewed for a permanent position at the bank. I did not get that job but she recommended me for another position. Ellen and I had never met prior to the interview, but her recommendation was so strong that throughout the interviews for the other position, people kept asking, "Are you the person from Ellen Hope?" Ms Hope gave me access and I got the job. God bless Ellen Hope for giving me hope!

Then came Naz Vahid! When I had no voice, this woman used hers to be a voice for me. Several years into my career, I had been interviewed for a higher position at the bank and was rejected because someone in a decision-making position had said I was "not X Bank material".

That statement was meant to be a closed door, a final decision. But Naz stepped in and challenged the person who made the pronouncement. She was so passionate, and took it so personal that I had to ask, "Why does she care so much?"

It was later I found out that Naz had had a similar challenge, in which a former boss had told her he did not think she could have a particular position. She had been upset and had told him, "One day, you will report to me", and he did! So when she heard the reason I was rejected, she fought for me, and I got the job! God bless Naz Vahid!

INDELIBLE IMPRESSIONS

I learned two things from that experience. The first is that you don't have to agree with a bad opinion or negative feedback. You can use it as fuel and energy to prove the person wrong by exceeding expectations through hard work and discipline. Secondly, you can be a voice for other people who may not be in a position to push back.

Those who have been blessed with benevolence and grace should not keep it to themselves. We can and should turn around and share that same grace with others. Personally, I believe that the only way to thank God and thank the human angels who have helped us is to help others. Speak for others; use your position to help others.

To sum it all up, the grace of God took this African immigrant, who had started as a temporary employee, to be elevated to the highest position at the bank, the most coveted position of Managing Director. Grace and grace alone made this possible!

CONCLUSION

THANKFUL, GRATEFUL, EXPECTANT...

So, it has been a story of grace all the way. Some say grace is unmerited favor; others say grace is getting things we did not work for or earn. I agree with all those. And I would like to add that grace is the hand of God. Almost always, when I wake up and say my prayers, it often starts with giving thanks. Yes, deliberate acts of recounting the goodness of God. We also do this as a family when we say our family prayers.

I am grateful for the grace of God in my life and I am expectant of the grace of God that is yet to unfold. The next few pages were deliberately left blank, as there are more chapters to be written in the future about the continuing grace of God.

Thankful, grateful and expectant. Grace, grace and then more grace!!!

ABOUT THE AUTHOR

Bola Crown is committed and passionate about empowering people into fulfilling their destinies. She is a motivational speaker, an inspirational speaker, a marriage, and career counselor.

With over 20 years corporate experience, cutting across two continents and several financial institutions, Bola uses her life experiences as a springboard in her speaking engagements.

Bola is a writer, with several articles published in magazines and online media outlets.

She has been invited to speak in several places including US, Canada and Nigeria.

Bola and her family share a love of traveling.

www.ingramcontent.com/pod-product-compliance
Lightning Source LLC
Chambersburg PA
CBHW071419040426
42445CB00012BA/1216